First World War
and Army of Occupation
War Diary
France, Belgium and Germany

66 DIVISION
197 Infantry Brigade
Headquarters
5 October 1915 - 17 February 1916

WO95/3134/1

The Naval & Military Press Ltd
www.nmarchive.com
Published in association with The National Archives

Published by

The Naval & Military Press Ltd

Unit 10 Ridgewood Industrial Park,

Uckfield, East Sussex,

TN22 5QE England

Tel: +44 (0) 1825 749494

www.naval-military-press.com

www.nmarchive.com

This diary has been reprinted in facsimile from the original. Any imperfections are inevitably reproduced and the quality may fall short of modern type and cartographic standards.

© Crown Copyright

Images reproduced by permission of The National Archives, London, England, 2015.

Contents

Document type	Place/Title	Date From	Date To
Heading	WO95/3134/1		
Heading	66th Division 197th Infy Bde Bde Headquarters 1915 Sep-1916 Feb 1917-Feb-1917 Jly		
Heading	66 Division HQ. 197 Bde 1915 Sep-1916 Dec		
War Diary	Camp Crowboro Sussex	05/10/1915	05/10/1915
War Diary	Tunbridge Wells	05/11/1915	05/01/1916
Heading	War Diary of 197th Infantry Brigade From February 1st To 29th February 1916 Volume I		
War Diary	Hartfield	02/02/1916	02/02/1916
War Diary	Tunbridge Wells	17/02/1916	17/02/1916
Miscellaneous	Remarks And References To Appendices	04/09/1915	04/09/1915

WO 95/31341/1

66TH DIVISION
197TH INFY BDE

BDE HEADQUARTERS
~~FEB - JLY 1917.~~

1915 SEP - 1916 FEB
1917 FEB - 1917 JLY

66 DIVISION

HQ 197 BDE

1915 SEP — 1916 DEC

3022

Army Form C. 2118

WAR DIARY
or
INTELLIGENCE SUMMARY
(Erase heading not required.)

Instructions regarding War Diaries and Intelligence Summaries are contained in F.S. Regs., Part II. and the Staff Manual respectively. Title Pages will be prepared in manuscript.

Place	Date	Hour	Summary of Events and Information	Remarks and references to Appendices
Camp. Crowboro' Sussex.	5/10/15	9 a.m.	The Brigade was seen at work by the General Officer Commanding 2nd. Army on 15.9.15. 3 Captains and 19 Subalterns from the 2/6th., 2/7th. and 2/8th. Battalions Lancashire Fusiliers have been despatched to join Imperial Service Units in the Dardanelles since the last Diary was sent in.	

[signature]

Colonel,

Commanding 197th. Infantry Brigade.

Army Form C. 2118

WAR DIARY
or
INTELLIGENCE SUMMARY.
(Erase heading not required.)

Instructions regarding War Diaries and Intelligence Summaries are contained in F. S. Regs., Part II. and the Staff Manual respectively. Title Pages will be prepared in manuscript.

Place	Date	Hour	Summary of Events and Information	Remarks and references to Appendices
Tunbridge Wells.	Nov. 5th. 1915	9 am.	Three Captains and fourteen Subalterns were dispatched to join the Imperial Service Units in the Dardanelles on 4th. October 1915. Three hundred rifles were dispatched to the 41st., 101st. and 108th. Provisional Batts. during the month of October, whilst 40 rifles were temporarily sent to the 66th. (East Lancs) Division R. F. A. 90,000 rounds of ammunition were sent out with these 300 rifles. The Brigade moved from Crowborough to Tunbridge Wells by march route on 21st. October 1915.	

W. Quinn, Colonel,
Commanding 197th. Infantry Brigade.

Army Form C. 2118

WAR DIARY
or
INTELLIGENCE SUMMARY
(Erase heading not required.)

Instructions regarding War Diaries and Intelligence Summaries are contained in F.S. Regs., Part II. and the Staff Manual respectively. Title Pages will be prepared in manuscript.

Place	Date	Hour	Summary of Events and Information	Remarks and references to Appendices
Tunbridge Wells	5/12/15	9 a.m.	Brigade Transport Inspection by Major General Landon C. B. Units of the Brigade inspected by General Dickson, Inspector General of Infantry. Units of the Brigade inspected by the Assistant Inspector of Gymnasia. Brig-General Beckett C. B., handed over Command of the Division to Major-General Blomfield C. B., D. S. O. All Japanese rifles and ammunition on charge despatched to Weedon, being replaced by Lee Enfield rifles and ammunition. Bandsmen returned to duty in the ranks. Lt-Colonel John Hall V. D., assumed command of the 3/5th. Batt. Lancs. Fusiliers. 1 officer (subaltern) 3/5th. Batt. Lancashire Fusiliers proceeded to join Imperial Service Unit in France No. 11735 Private George Howarth, 2/6th. Battalion Lancs. Fusiliers died of pneumonia on 28th. November. 1915. 144 and 118 recruits have been received for the 2/6th. & 3/5th. Batts. Lancashire Fusiliers respectively., during the month of November	

M. Munro, Colonel,
Commanding 197th. Infantry Brigade.

Army Form C. 2118

WAR DIARY
or
INTELLIGENCE SUMMARY
(Erase heading not required.)

Instructions regarding War Diaries and Intelligence Summaries are contained in F. S. Regs., Part II. and the Staff Manual respectively. Title Pages will be prepared in manuscript.

Place	Date	Hour	Summary of Events and Information	Remarks and references to Appendices
Tunbridge Wells.	5/1/16.	9-0am.	The Brigade was inspected by the G.O.C. 66th. (East Lancashire) Division on 10.12.15. He commented favourably on the steadiness and turn out of the men. Instructions were received during the past month to transfer to the G.O.C. Weedon 15 surplus rifles on charge of each Unit. This transaction has been completed except in the case of one Battalion which has been awaiting cases for the despatch of these rifles. These have now been received and they will be sent off at once. 40 Lee Enfield Rifles have been lent by the 3/5th. Battalion, under instructions received, to the Divisional Artillery, Forest Row. 800 rounds Lee Enfield Ammunition have also been transferred to that Unit by this Battalion.	

Colonel,
Commanding 197th. Infantry Brigade.

CONFIDENTIAL

WAR DIARY

of

197th INFANTRY BRIGADE

From February 1st to 29th February 1916.

VOLUME I

****

Army Form C. 2118

WAR DIARY
INTELLIGENCE SUMMARY
(Erase heading not required.)

Instructions regarding War Diaries and Intelligence Summaries are contained in F. S. Regs., Part II. and the Staff Manual respectively. Title Pages will be prepared in manuscript.

Place	Date	Hour	Summary of Events and Information	Remarks and references to Appendices
Hartfield	2.2.16	12 noon	Concentration March of Divisional 1st. line Transport and Field Ambulance	nil
Tunbridge Wells.	17.2.16	10 a.m.	The 2/7th. Battalion Lancashire Fusiliers were seen at their ordinary drill and work by the G.O.C. 2nd. Army C.F.	nil

M. Guinin
Colonel
Commanding 197th. Infantry Brigade.

Army Form C. 2118

WAR DIARY
or
INTELLIGENCE SUMMARY
(Erase heading not required.)

Instructions regarding War Diaries and Intelligence Summaries are contained in F. S. Regs., Part II. and the Staff Manual respectively. Title Pages will be prepared in manuscript.

Place	Date	Hour	Summary of Events and Information	Remarks and references to Appendices
Tunbridge Wells.	4/2/16.	9-0 a.m.	The 3/5th. Batt. Lan. Fus. was seen at their ordinary drill and work by the G.O.C. 2nd. Army on the 27th. January. 1916.	

[signature] Colonel,

Commanding 197th. Infantry Brigade.

197th Lancashire Fusiliers Brigade

REMARKS AND REFERENCES TO APPENDICES.

(c) ORGANIZATION FOR DEFENCE.

The Brigade is at present armed with 2,400 Japanese Rifles, the 2/6th. 2/7th. and 2/8th. Battalions Lancashire Fusiliers still hold a total of 400 Japanese Rifles on charge for the 3/5th. Battalion, which has so many recruits and are still so few in number as not to be able to make use of them. For the present this Battalion is armed with 200 Japanese Rifles.

AMMUNITION.

The four Battalions of the Brigade hold among them the following:-

Japanese	Service Ammunition	720,000	rounds
..	Practice ..	2,682	..
Lee Enfield	.. ..	1,394	..
Machine Gun	.. ..	33,600	..

(d) TRAINING

The training of the Brigade suffers considerably from the greatly reduced establishment of the Battalions, — The number of Divisional and other duties, and the fact that Officers and N.C.Os are constantly withdrawn for special classes of instruction, which, useful though they are, interfere materially with the systematic training of Units. The training areas are admirable for Field Training and there are excellent rifle ranges available. The recruits course with the Japanese rifle has now been commenced by all Units. The three weeks entrenching work on the South London defences has had a remarkable effect in improving the physique of the men.

(e) DISCIPLINE

Conduct is good. There is a good and soldierly spirit throughout the Battalions of the Brigade.

(f) (i) ADMINISTRATION

There is still a great shortage of Medical drugs, necessaries etc. The health of the men however, is decidedly good.

(iii) Supply Service quite satisfactory

(iv) Transport services satisfactory. The draught horses and limber wagons mentioned in last month's Diary are of great service. There is at present only one water cart in the Brigade. 41 more pack mules have been received making 77 in all. All of these are still without any equipment.

(v) Storage for Small Arm Ammunition is very much needed. At present every Battalion of the Brigade has a considerable quantity of ammunition stored in one of the wooden huts which would be extremely dangerous in the event of fire in the Camp.

(vi) BILLETING AND HUTTING
The hutting accommodation is very good except that nearly all the huts leak badly in wet weather of which there has been a great deal, of late. The water supply is still very insufficient.

(ix) SUPPLY OF REMOUNTS
    10 more of these have been received since the last Diary was sent in. All the Battalions are however, still under strength in respect of both Officers Chargers and Draught Horses.

(h) PREPARATION OF UNITS FOR IMPERIAL SERVICE
    The establishment of the 2/6th., 2/7th., and 2/8th. Batts. Lancashire Fusiliers still remains 600. The strength of the 3/5th. Battn. Lancs. Fusiliers is still only about a third of even that establishment.

[signature]
Colonel,
Commanding 197th. Infantry Brigade.

Crowborough.
    September 4th. 1915.

www.ingramcontent.com/pod-product-compliance
Lightning Source LLC
Chambersburg PA
CBHW081517160426
43193CB00014B/2720